AMERICA'S
THIRD
CENTURY

AMERICA'S THIRD CENTURY

Norman Macrae
Deputy Editor of *The Economist*

HARCOURT BRACE JOVANOVICH, INC.
New York Chicago San Francisco Atlanta

Cover *Washington at Verplanck's Point* by John Trumbull.
Courtesy, The Henry Francis du Pont Winterthur Museum.

This survey by Norman Macrae first appeared as a special
supplement to *The* London *Economist* on October 25, 1975.
© The Economist Newspaper Ltd., London, 1975

ISBN: 0-15-502609-7

Library of Congress Catalog Card Number: 76-1532

Printed in the United States of America

PREFACE

In this survey (originally published in *The Economist*, October 25, 1975) I have followed my usual journalistic habit of pinching without attribution and then personally embellishing (usually just beyond recognition) the best ideas of all my friends. No one of them will conceivably agree with all of the mixture of forecasts that comes out. At the assembly of the World Future Society I again raided the fertile minds of Herman Kahn (who always quantifies admirably what I only feel), Professor Dan Bell, and a lot of others. The best figures of the past with which to illumine the future now come from John McHale (both from his *World Facts and Trends*, published by Macmillan, and from his unpublished policy study on "Human Requirements," which is obtainable from the Center for Integrated Studies at Binghamton, N.Y.).

In New York City I was particularly indebted to the wise and balanced Professor Sidney Rolfe (and to the apartment full of New York intellectuals he invited to a party for me to quiz), to the flashing mind of John Diebold (for whose Institute of Public Policy Studies I have done some past work, so our ideas do become a little intermingled), and to my friends at the Sloan

Foundation. The Americans have a habit of setting up privately backed or even official committees to collect diverse views on practically everything. America's leading intellectuals submit to them typewritten documents that are labelled "confidential" but then handed to anybody on request. Newspapermen tell me that this means you can purloin all their best ideas provided you never reveal which intellectuals dared to utter them, because they are all liable to be attached to some presidential candidate next time and attribution could be embarrassing. I have taken advantage of this convention with enthusiasm.

Norman Macrae

CONTENTS

RECESSIONAL FOR THE SECOND GREAT EMPIRE?

The two hundred years since the United States won their fortuitous victory in their Revolutionary War have been the two centuries of the world's material advance. It is probable that three centuries of material advance will be all that is needed. For the first 10,000 years of man's existence as a producing animal—from about 8000 BC when commercial agricultural cultivation probably began, down to about 1776—people did not grow much richer. By 2076 people sensibly may not want to grow much richer, but for quite a few years yet most people most definitely will.

And this is a main reason for worry at America's 200th birthday. There is a danger that the Americans, with all their power for dynamism and good, may be about to desert what should be their manifest and now rather easy destiny of leading the rest of us towards a decent world society and an abundant cheap lunch. If they do, the leadership of the world may be yielded from American to less sophisticated hands, at a perilous moment.

During research for this survey the fears listed here seemed to me to be (a) obvious, (b) avertible, (c) not recognised by nine-tenths of the Americans to whom I spoke. Indeed, the largest cohorts of very intelligent Americans are looking for their favourite fears in precisely the opposite directions.

This sets a problem about the order in which the arguments in this survey should be set down. It is a pity to begin by clodhopping on corns. The survey's main arguments are that:

(1) The two great empires that have ruled the first two centuries of industrial advance—the British in 1776–1876, and the American in 1876–1976—have handled the task of world leadership surprisingly well. But the Americans on the eve of 1976 are showing the same symptoms of a drift from dynamism as the British did at the end of their century in 1876.

(2) World leadership is therefore liable to pass into new hands quite early in the century 1976–2076. During this century the world will face some extraordinary opportunities, and also some bizarre dangers.

(3) The opportunities will probably include an ability to put material living standards in the twenty-first century more or less wherever men want them. I explain later why I think that the remarkable upturn in around 1776 in all of this survey's charts will continue (indeed, probably accelerate) for a while, and why I share the

Post 1776 take-off

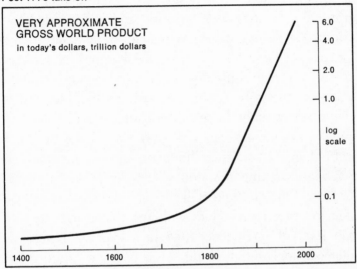

**VERY APPROXIMATE
GROSS WORLD PRODUCT**
in today's dollars, trillion dollars

6.0

4.0

2.0

1.0

log
scale

0.1

1400   1600   1800   2000

Smoothed trend ignoring some decades zigzags

Hudson Institute's guess (1) * that mankind could trans-
form its present annual gross world product (gwp) of
around $5½ trillion made by 4 billion people to, some
time within the lifetime of kids already adolescent, a
"satiating" gwp of between $100 trillion and $350 trillion for a world population of between 10 billion and 30
billion people. Somewhere in that range (perhaps between about twice and five times today's average American income per head for everybody) men may stop
growing much richer because they will no longer want
to grow much richer.

(4) During these next few years, however, the bizarre

* Numbers in parentheses refer to notes at the back of the book.

3

dangers will include the destructive (because quite small groups of fanatics and terrorists and even individual criminals will very soon have the capability of destroying the planet) and, for example, the biophysical (2) (because the present orthodox method of creating a human being—namely, by copulation between two individuals giving no thought to what the product will be—may quite soon change). Sex is already 99.99% for fun, and technology is bound to home in on the pre-planned twice-in-a-lifetime occasion when it will be for reproduction. Our children will probably "progressively" be able to order their babies with the shape and strength and level of intelligence that they choose, as well as alter existing human beings so as to insert artificial intelligence, retune brains, change personality, modify moods, control behaviour. And lots of even more horrid things like that. The pace and sophistication with which some of these things are not done will hang on the world's leading nations, whom other peoples will most wish to emulate or will most fear to fall behind. It will be very desirable to retain strong and calm American influence in this period, rather than to yield all of world leadership to (at best) the inexperienced Japanese.

(5) America's contribution in its third century will depend largely on how its three main institutions evolve in or out of pace with the changing times. These three main institutions are, in reverse order of importance: its business corporations; its government; and its mechanisms for living together (what takes over from church,

family, pioneer spirit, small-town togetherness, the prob-
ably-failed experiment of suburbia—during a century
when the third and greatest transport revolution, that of
telecommunications, should gradually allow an increasing number of breadwinners to live in whatever communities they wish to form and to telecommute daily
into their New York offices from homes in Tahiti or the
Alps).

This summary has set a lot of angels dancing on the
point of a pin. It may seem clumsy to try to pick out the
pattern of the dance by first brooding on what may happen to American business during these next few years.
But I think that the influence of this might be decisive
for the lifetime of my children, just as what happened to
British and then American business in the years immediately after 1776 and 1876 largely shaped the two centuries 1776–1876 and 1876–1976.

At one stage of my journey through America in 1975,
this thought made me rather glum.

AMERICA JOINS THE FABIAN SOCIETY

America is adopting many of the upper-class snob habits that checked Britain's economic dynamism after 1876. Such as anti-business paternalism, a glorification of gamekeepers . . .

The first century of material advance after 1776, based on the invention of steam power and the transport revolution of the railways, was led by Great Britain. During this period it was widely understood that God was an Englishman because the most efficient businessmen temporarily were.

The British century ended in around 1876 as it became apparent that the most efficient businessmen now weren't. The second century of material advance from 1876–1976, based on the invention of manufacturers' assembly line techniques and the transport revolution of the internal combustion engine, was therefore led by the United States. There were societal, psychological and technological reasons why America was ready in 1876 to take over industrial leadership from old Britain. Awkwardly, these same reasons can be cited in 1975 to suggest that old America may be about to give up that leadership to somebody else.

The chief reason why 1876 ushered in America's century was that entrepreneurs' verve was by then most likely to sprout in that nation so largely self-selected from families enterprising enough to have migrated across the wide ocean, and yet new enough not yet to have created the aristocratic or jealous or intellectual institutions which castigate moneymaking as *infra dig* or unfair. The surge into the Henry Ford revolution should have been as organisable in the Britain of 1876 as in the America. What was missing in Britain by that moralising Gladstone's and that do-gooding Disraeli's day was the incentive provided by any accordance of social standing to business panache.

Remember how easy the surge after 1876 was—just as, for different reasons, see below, I am going to maintain that a much bigger surge after 1976 is also going to be. Our grandfathers lived in a time when any bankworthy member of the middle class anywhere with a good entrepreneurial idea could expect to be profiting from it (and to have set course to change the world?) within a few months. The Ford Motor Company was founded in mid-June, 1903, with a cash capital equal to today's price of a small suburban house and only 125 employees; it sold its first cars to customers that October, and made a profit from then on (3). Yet between 1876–1910—while America was rearing Rockefeller,

Morgan, Harriman, Carnegie, Frick and Ford to seize this new age of opportunity—what single name of a new and domestically based British entrepreneur springs easily to mind?

The main reason for Britain's entrepreneurial decay around 1876 was that a century's experience as top dog had by then become debilitating. The British upper class was strengthening its gut feeling that new sorts of commerce were surely rather vulgar, while the British business-decision-making class had itself become bureaucratic and protectionist rather than entrepreneurial. As each new technological development appeared in the late 19th century there were interests in Britain (entrenched among employers as well as in craft unions) who had prospered from the development which it would replace, so they united to wish that the new idea would please go away. America gained also because its industrial revolution was from the start based on technology geared to the market, as Edison and the half-million other American patentees of 1870–1900 sought dynamically to devise conveniences for the many instead of to dredge up ideas fascinating to the few. By contrast the British industrial revolution had even originally been based on more leisurely and gentlemanly science, as scholars like Newton and Watt looked at an apple or a kettle and then thought of a most ingenious wheeze.

America's entrepreneurial verve instead of Britain's businesses' bureaucracy, America's output-oriented technology instead of Britain's scientific curiosity whether the moon was made of green cheese, America's bloody-clawed capitalism instead of Britain's good corporate citizenship whose attempt at paternalism was bound to fall down a class and generation gap. In 1876 those were young America's strengths, while these were old Britain's senescent disease.

And today? The Briton travelling through America in 1975 at first has the eerie feeling that he has gone back to when grandfather knew H. G. Wells. The entrepreneurial fervour of the industrial age seems to be dying in the west. I think (see later in this survey) that this first impression is too gloomy, but it will be good neighbourliness first to rub America's birthday nose into the warning signs.

TREASON OF THE CLERKS

The bad news for the world's teeming masses this bicentennial is that in America the whole concept of thrustful business is in danger of becoming unloved. The intellectuals have joined in the sneering against it, making it fashionable to believe that stagnation is not only wise but clever. This is exactly how it was when Britain's post-1876 decline began. It is strange that peoples do not see that not learning from history is bunk.

Through most of history, businessmen have been told by the upper classes of society that they are pushful upstarts. Since businessmen want most to rise in society, this has naturally often discouraged them from starting to push up. As even de Tocqueville said in the patchy book which many Americans regard as their national legitimation, the church in the late middle ages provided the first hope of a dynamic challenge to the old stagnant feudalism—as the clergy opened its ranks to all classes, to the poor and the rich, to the villein and the lord, to every uppity Becket. But by the time societies were rich enough for top churchmen to have a nice life, provided nobody disturbed them, the church comfortably joined itself to the rest of the establishment in deprecating restless change, although it still good-naturedly said it was in favour of succour of the poor.

The breakthrough towards continuing material advance therefore waited on the emergence of another part of the upper class which was ready to reassure the lively that panache was respectable. This new class came in England in the 17th century when King Charles II favoured intellectuals interested in the scientific method, perhaps because he sought male company among an establishment different from that which had lost his father his head. After a century's slow germination, intellectuals in ferment played a major part in awakening Britain in the first seven-eighths of its 1776–1876 century—agricultural innovators against the squires, freetraders against the mercantilism of governments, and doctors who favoured a chemical feast against opponents of some advances like chloroform. Then, just after the mid-19th-century, this new British ginger group followed the old church into favouring a decent gentlemanly stagnation.

By around 1876 a British intellectual could have a pleasant life in contemplation, and his most natural resentment (like the resentment of the squire, the parson and the bureaucrat) came to be against vulgar people who were restlessly and commercially pushful. After about 1876 a "progressive intellectual" in British public life no longer meant a person who believed in progress and change; no longer a person who was eager to rout down to the roots of every way of doing things, so as to cut and graft wherever an improvement in production or effectiveness or competitiveness or individual liberty could be secured. A "progressive intellectual" meant a paternalist, who did not like change very much but was eager to pass on in welfare benefits a larger part of the easy growth in national income which his own anti-growth attitudes now made it slightly more difficult to attain.

And that is exactly what has happened in America in these years just before 1976. The United States has joined the Fabian Society of about 1903. Many of the new Democrat members of Congress, including some presidential aspirants, would find that Fabian Society their most natural home, militant middle-class feminism and all, but plus the old American disease. When upper class Americans impose snob values on emotional populists, they often think that they have gotten religion—and catch the lynching spirit.

It would be impertinent for a foreigner to object to America's creeping ethic of anti-dynamism if it had merely sprung from American selfishness. When you have a gnp per head over $7,000 a year, you naturally begin to regard growing much richer as a bit of a bore—although American Christians and humanists should be reminding zero-growth Americans that, by discontinuing their own industrial dynamism which has helped so much to drive world technology up through the bud, they could cruelly reduce the forward prospects of the 2 billion angry people on incomes under $200 a year with whom we share this rather small planet (4). But the real horror today is that America is not going slowly stagnationist out of selfishness. On campuses across the continent, a peculiarly innumerate anti-growth cult is being taught to a generation of idealistic kids as if it was high moral philosophy, or even a religion.

INDUSTROPHOBIA

This is a familiar fault in that otherwise lovely, brave continent. Remember G. K. Chesterton?

There is nothing the matter with Americans except their ideals. The real American is all right; it is the ideal American who is all wrong. (5)

Idealist Americans should ponder the delay they caused to the trans-Alaska oil pipeline, without humbug.

There can be no real pretence this delay was motivated by any environmentalists' thoughtful belief that the 15 square miles covered by this pipeline would spoil the view of the other 599,985 square miles of Alaskan wilderness (6) which are hardly looked at by anybody anyway (the few adventurous tourists who do travel through this wilderness will certainly detour deliberately to what will be the pipeline's slightly contrasting and therefore mildly interesting sight). There can also be no pretence that, at least after its initial redesign, the pipeline will be unfair to local wildlife; for them it will be an occasionally-useful shelter from the Arctic wind. Instead, the delay stemmed from a desire to be nasty to oil companies, plus aristocratic resentment that poorer people growing richer can become more uncouth. The delay could have been justified if it had been used to make the pipeline's building less of a drunkards' gold rush, less expensive, more integrated with the community. But, of course, the costs and urgency created by the delay made each of these factors worse.

It was an unforeseen misfortune that this spasm of industrophobia should have come at a time when the delay to oil pipements has certainly cut America's employment, has certainly aggravated the oil crisis for the energy-short destitute countries, has necessitated shabby compromises in American foreign policy. In order to make more symmetrical an Alaskan view for practically nobody, the unemployment of black teenagers in New York City has been pushed up the last few percentage points towards 40%, a few tens of thousands more brown men have starved to death in Bangladesh, and several hundred thousand Israeli families have been put in greater danger. It would be vindictive to hammer home these truths to the hangdog, but there still aren't any hangdogs. It was eerie during my trip across the campuses of the continent to hear so many supposedly left-wing young Americans who still thought they were expressing an entirely new and progressive philosophy as they mouthed the same prejudices as Trollope's 19th century Tory squires: attacking any further expansion of industry and commerce as impossibly vulgar, because ecologically unfair to their pheasants and wild ducks. Some of their emotions were rather nicely expressed. The upper class has always had the ability to sound persuasive while being fatuous, to dress gamekeepers' selfishness in pretty witty phrases. At this fin de siècle that mood is infecting the Americans, the upper class of the world. It needs to be turned back.

It can be turned back. But awkwardly, America in 1975 is also suffering from two other symptoms of Britain's post-1876 disease.

THE
RETREAT
FROM
MR EDISON

Two other dangers: America has bureau-cratised its technology, and very nearly its business too.

Science is the thing that was nurtured in Britain under Charles II, and has been encrusting in post-Caroline cobwebs ever since. A scientist seeks kudos by advancing the frontiers of knowledge, and if you ask him whether he is probing the frontiers that most need to be advanced then you are some sort of a slob. Technology is the thing that was nurtured in America in the days of Eli Whitney and Edison, and in those days it meant a search for the innovations that would be most saleable. In Japan it still means that.

But in modern America, while a scientist seeks kudos, a technologist now searches for something called funding. A large part of funding comes directly or indirectly from the federal government.

17

I met a man in Washington who makes a living studying political utterances and forecasting which sorts of technology will find politicians to be an easy touch over various periods ahead. He claims his profession is right 60% of the time, and bought me a drink because he said he had prospered through long practising what he kindly called "Macrae's law" which I had much later preached in *The Economist*. This is that:

> *In modern conditions of high elasticity of both production and substitution, we will generally create a temporary but large surplus of whatever the majority of decision-influencing people five or ten years earlier believed was going to be in most desperately short supply. This is because the well-advertised views of the decision-influencers tend to be believed by both profit-seeking private producers and consensus-following governments, and these two then combine to cause excessive production of precisely the things that the decision-influencers had been saying would be most obviously needed.* (7)

Thus when Russia beat America with a sputnik into space in 1957, everybody in Washington cried that America would be left in a "missile gap" behind Russia for the rest of the century. This meant that America would hurriedly and expensively produce a vast and unnecessary surplus of much better rockets than the Russians, and that the big technological programme for the 1960s would be to fire this surplus off at the moon.

As the American government now directly or indirectly finances more scientific research every few months than took place in all the world in all the 1923 years of the Christian era before I was born, I naturally had a yen to believe that these billions of dollars which could shape my children's futures were distributed on principles more firmly-founded than those of a bad joke which I had once made up in my bath. I burrowed like a squirrel round America to find those principles, but must report that I could find only nuts.

LAND OF LOW INVESTMENT

There is an Office of Technology Assessment in the Washington phonebook, so I rang it to find the principles on which it works. It turns out to be the opposite of what its name says. It is a taxpayer-financed ecologists' organisation, created for anti-technology assessment.

If you invent a better mousetrap in America, then this committee with formidable left-wing ladies (see later) is authorised to inquire whether this might be environmentally unfair to mice. Fortunately, the office has no money, so cannot actually do anything; but this chase after moonbeams has reached the dangerously earnest stage where its literature is no longer entirely written by kooks.

The discouragement of investment in new technology in American profit-making industry (as distinct from in politicians' latest emotional spasms) is worrying because it is a dowse that is being banged on an already spluttering light. For the last 25 years America's investment has been a lower % of gnp than any other industrial country's except Britain's. On one definition it has fallen even behind Britain's. During the third quarter of the twentieth century America's output per manhour in manufacturing doubled—but it quadrupled in some other industrial countries, and multiplied by nine in Japan; even Britain slightly exceeded America's poor performance (see chart).

This is changing the world at about the same speed as it was changed early in Britain's post-1876 decline. A swift deterioration, but with long trails of imperial glory

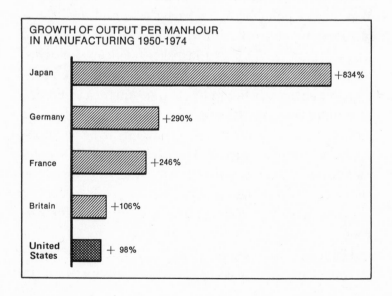

GROWTH OF OUTPUT PER MANHOUR
IN MANUFACTURING 1950-1974

Japan +834%
Germany +290%
France +246%
Britain +106%
United States + 98%

still. In 1960, the distant year for whose figures Dr Edward Denison (8) produced by far the best international comparison of productivity, America enjoyed a living standard approximately twice as high as that of northwest Europe. Denison attributed about a quarter of this gap to the fact that America then had more capital equipment per worker in industry. In much of manufacturing and the large parts of investment affected by bureaucratic decision, I think that this American advantage has now nearly gone; but in the service industries, which should be much more important in future, the American worker probably does usually have a better programmed computer behind him.

Nearly another quarter of the Denison gap in 1960 came because American workers were better educated and better deployed in workplaces with large economies of scale. In manufacturing I think that some of this advantage has now gone. America's enthusiasm for general higher education (with 56% of its high school girls and 58% of its high school boys now going on to post-secondary education) probably is not providing as many skilled craftsmen as continental Europe's apprenticeship system. If the Europeans do now have more suitable workers using a more quickly growing stock of therefore more modern machines, then America's relative decline in manufacturing should be expected to continue fast. But American (eg) banks still seem to me more efficient than European banks, especially as they now have so many able ex-postgraduate-students about.

21

And that leads to "Denison's residual," which accounted for most of America's lead over Europe in 1960. This was Europe's "lag in the application of knowledge" and "general efficiency," so that, as I said in my last study of America in 1969:

> North-west Europe's real output per worker in 1960 was only approximately the same as America's in 1925, although by 1960 Europe's workers were much better educated than American workers had been in 1925—and had of course a far more advanced technology to draw on. The implication is that there is some long-standing, history-given, go-getting element in America's culture which Europeans and others have been unable to imitate. (9)

In that study I searched America for this residual, and thought that I found it in the greater instinct of Americans, shown equally by the American engineer in the factory and the American housewife in the kitchen, to say: "now here is the problem, how can I solve it by a systematic approach?" On this trip I searched for it again.

It is still there when Americans are allowed to make individual decisions. But an increasing number of decisions in America are now being caught up in bureaucratic nets instead. In business this applies particularly to ventures into new fields. If you are introducing a new product in America, then the order of operation is laid down as (1) recognition of need, (2) proposal of design,

(3) verification of design concept . . . and so on to stage number umpteen. All those departments and layers of management in big corporations then insist on being consulted at every stage, building up their empires of staff to meet the extra work which they create for themselves. This is serious because half the non-food products in the supermarkets of rich countries did not exist in precisely that form ten years ago, and half those on sale now will have been replaced by competitors in ten years' time. One reason for the growth of American multinational subsidiaries abroad is that they provide top management with the fatal option of the easy let-out; it is simpler to say "let's repeat this set-up and lay-out in

Post 1776 take-off

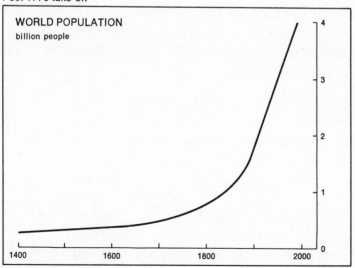

Brazil" than to go through all the hierarchical pains of a brand new investment project each time you want to look expansive.

Consultants report that American firms reach initial decisions about investment more quickly than the Japanese, but then take much longer to bring them into effect. The increasing time between the beginning and completion of any task in American business—which Professor Kenneth Galbraith (10) thinks is an "imperative of technology" and a sign of the need for planning—is in fact a sign of increase in bureaucratisation and of the need for America to escape from economic planning back to paying more attention to a rapidly changing market.

The wheel has come full circle since the generation of Rockefeller, Carnegie and Henry Ford. In 1965–1975 what name of a new and domestically-based American entrepreneur springs to mind? Even Britain has produced more Jim Slaters.

MANAGEMENT DOESN'T EXIST

In the mid-1960s, shortly after people had grown tired of saying that America was bound to pull ever further ahead of Europe because of a "technology gap" (even though America was investing a smaller % of gnp than any continental European country), it became fashionable to say that America was bound to pull ever further ahead of Europe because of a "management gap" (ie, America had elevated management into a science). It has now been discovered, however, that management science does not exist except in the following ingenious sense.

Big American corporations will often centralise their policy-making (11), and get a significant initial gain in effectiveness; but then, as time passes, will find that this does not work because the central planners do not know what is really going on out in the field. So these corporations will then decentralise, and get a significant initial gain in effectiveness, but will then find that all their divisions are going in different directions. So they will then recentralise, and get a significant gain in effectiveness, but after a time . . .

This constant reorganisation is in fact very sensible, and is a main reason why I judge that big American corporations are still often the most efficient day-to-day business operators (though not investors) in the world. European and Japanese companies do not keep their executives on their toes by reorganising nearly as frequently, and governments do not have the opportunity to do so. This is one reason why governments are such inefficient operators. In many of them you nowadays have at the same time all the disadvantages of centralisation (because cabinet ministers are signing bits of paper that have no relevance to what is actually going on) and decentralisation (because what is actually going on is diverging impossibly in a dozen different directions at once).

Still, the present American corporation management system—of chop a little and change a lot—is a device for dealing with the problems set by bureaucracy, not for replacing it by entrepreneurship. In a search for entrepreneurship American corporations have passed in recent decades through phases of being led at one stage by engineers (who tend to disregard both balance sheets and people), then by super-salesmen (whom the general public nowadays find absurd), and then by accountants.

There is no doubt that America has gained briefly from the age of the rule of accountants. The visiting economic journalist is still bedazzled by the way in which he can get from a quite junior employee in an American corporation more sensible and detailed statistical answers about cash flow targets, about what sales and profit trends as between different products are, than he can usually get at very top levels in equivalent British companies. It must be a continuing advantage to American corporations that they know what they at least think they are trying to do.

Nevertheless, I believe that the age of the rule by accountants is ending, for two reasons. First, in an age of inflation, the units in which they think they work have proved to be units that are too easily fiddled in order to fool stockholders (which may not matter) and fool themselves (which does matter). Secondly, the mode of organisation favoured by the accountant-presidents has been the old hierarchical mode. The hierarchical system served America well in the manufacturing age, when every engineering boss from Henry Ford down could arrange with precision what the person immediately below him did with his hands. But now that most Americans are white collar workers, each corporation executive is finding to his surprise that it is less easy to sit trying to arrange what the person below him should do with his imagination.

In ten years' time, my guess is that the accountants will be departing from the top, and will be succeeded by . . . perhaps the packagers of technology for transfer to the places that can most economically use it, but more probably by the organisers of incentives.

THE
WAY
OUT

*How America's business corporations
might survive.*

American business corporations therefore face three problems: dynamism is becoming unloved at home (and is called imperialism abroad), there is bureaucratisation of technology and partly of business. Earnest Swedes are making efficient straight assembly lines run round in deliberately less efficient circles, in order to try to make business more popular. It will be a misfortune for the hungry half of the world if America also comes to believe that the problems of its dying manufacturing age can thus best be met by an unproductivity drive.

The key strategies for American business corporations should be (1) to move the boring manufacturing jobs down to the poor south of the world, at maximum profit to both the poor south and themselves; (2) to redesign their domestic structures to fit the new knowledge-processing, unobsequious, post-manufacturing age.

Manufacturing is going to continue its march out of America anyway, much faster than you think. In 1900, about 43% of America's workforce was in the two largest employments of agriculture and domestic service; that proportion is down below 5% now. Today only about 23% of America's workforce is in manufacturing, and I expect it to drop to below 5% over the next few decades.

Awkwardly, at this moment when America's main exports should be of jobs and technology, America's main mechanism for exporting jobs and technology has run crazy. While novelists write best-sellers predicting that by 2020 the world will be ruled by six giant American multinational corporations, the day of the big multinationals is now likely to be ending.

END OF MULTINATIONALS?

Probably because the accountant-presidents predicted the future by extrapolating the past, the originally sensible device of the American multinational corporation has surged out of its cost controls. Compared with the moneymaking method of selling the knowhow through some licensing arrangement, the establishment of a multinational subsidiary was supposed to have the great advantage of maintaining ownership of the use of the process for the dear old firm; but multinational corporations failed to notice that, just as their emigrant boom took off, such material ownership was becoming no longer a source of economic power. (12)

The Americans brought to poorer countries their best equipment, together with the knowledge how to operate it in order to make the goods they previously exported, plus their own capital and managerial skill (which proved to be either copiable or untransplantable). All parts of this system looked tailormade to turn America's balance of payments towards deficit, although multinational corporations were profitable only so long as the dollar was overvalued—ie, so long as the Americans were expected to have a strong balance of payments.

A multinational corporation has now become a device for taking up an artificially weak bargaining posture versus the host government (which is able to say that the American company can open only in some high-unemployment area to which native manufacturers won't go); versus Marxists in the local parliament and ivory towers (who genuinely believe that giant multinational corporations wield some strange mesoeconomic power); versus the trade unions back home in America (who are liable at any moment to launch a worldwide strike against an American multinational on the grounds that it is being unfair by exporting jobs to workers in lower wage countries, who will then join the strike in order to get higher wages and thus export their own jobs back to America again); versus local business competitors, whose normal practices (tax-dodging in Latin European countries, giving bribes and arranging occasional coups d'état in poor countries) have to some extent to be copied for survival by the multinationals, who are then castigated by American congressional committees and the world's press.

There is one group of countries whose labour force is paid far below the standard of productivity appropriate to its high education (because its non-market-oriented economic system has made its entrepreneurship so inefficient), and where there is no danger of the trade unions turning bolshie. These are the bolshevik countries of Russia and east Europe. But the American system of technology transfer by multinationals has made it politically difficult to transfer American knowhow with good profit there, and has inhibited transfers to many of the poor countries (except about a half-dozen which are temporarily very well-ruled and about another dozen which are very corrupt). Also multinationals' executives often don't like living in poor dictatorships, and when they do there is a danger that their expatriate living habits in ex-colonial milieus can brutalise the society. At the back of every multinational's mind is the thought that in one of the 50 or so coups d'état in poor countries during the next three years, some incoming government is likely eventually to execute the presidents of all local American multinationals, probably very slowly in the public square as a populist spectator sport. The state department will then issue a protest. So American manufacturing multinationals have gone especially to west-

Post 1776 take-off

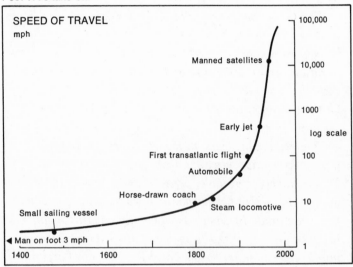

Reprinted with permission of Macmillan Publishing Co., Inc., from *World Facts and Trends,* Second Edition, by John McHale. © copyright 1972 by John McHale.

ern Europe, which was the next-richest area to America and therefore the next where manufacturing was bound to become uneconomic once Europe had stopped importing the temporary migrant workers to whom the natives were unfriendly but on whom European manufacturing relied.

EVERYBODY AS ENTREPRENEUR?

I stick to what I forecast in *The Economist* in 1971:

> As a prototype for the most successful sorts of firm in 30
> or 40 years' time, it may be most sensible to visualise
> small groups of organisers of systems designers, all living
> in their own comfortable homes in pleasant parts of the
> world and communicating with others in the group (and
> with the systems designers) by picturephone: arranging
> for the telecommunication of the latest best computerised
> learning programme on how to make a better mouse-trap
> (or, more probably, how to make the next-successor-but-
> five to integrated circuits) rooftop to rooftop to about
> 2,000 quickly trainable, even if only newly literate,
> workers assembled before their two-way-teaching-in com-
> puter terminals by some just tolerably efficient organis-
> ing subcontractor (also taught by long-distance telecom-
> municated computer lessons) in West Africa or Pakistan.
> (13)

That, however, raises a problem.

America invented powerful manufacturing business corporations in the first or 1876–1925 half of its past century, the half one can call the Carnegie–Ford corporation age; but I have just argued that in the years ahead manufacturing will be most profitable if operated out of the world's poor south. American business spread dynamism round the world in the second or 1926–1975 half of its past century, the half one can call the multinational corporation age; but I have just argued that this age is now ending.

American business corporations will therefore need to lead the world in their third revolution into a new mode within a century. The requirement for the knowledge-processing age will be to become the most efficient incentive-offerers to get a generation of very highly-educated Americans to use their imaginations, instead of being the most efficient at supervising how American non-operators don't turn a screw. The mode that most appeals to me is one of John Diebold's concepts of perhaps gradually making American business corporations more into "confederations of entrepreneurs" (14).

In the most extreme version of this very broad idea (and the most extreme versions seem to me the most probable, as witness what happened with Carnegie-Ford corporations and then with multi-nationals), a big business corporation would codify the costs and output required from its existing departments: transport department, typing pools, etc.

Then individuals or groups within the corporation could bid if they thought they could produce the stipulated output more competitively than the existing department did. If the tenders looked sensible, they could either take over the job on one of the sorts of contract discussed below, or (more usually at first) compete with the existing departments.

Some contracts for the internal entrepreneurs could sometimes be "very entrepreneurial"; eg, pay you something much less than your existing salaries, but the new typing pool which you are running—which would be able to sub-contract work out and in—would be a subsidiary company 49% owned by you. It could eventually

Post 1776 take-off

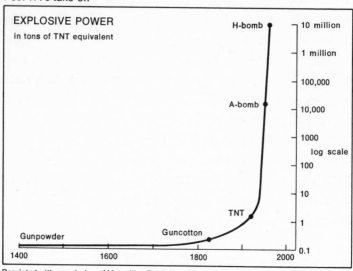

be sold, making you millionaires if you prove to have struck on a wheeze to make typing pools very much more productive in terms of what is actually wanted from them.

Other contracts could be almost-salaried (which would come to little more than a bid by a respected employee that he thought he could reorganise some function in the company better, so let him try, but at nearly full salary plus bonus if he succeeds).

Obviously new products, by-products and products the corporation has not thought of could most especially be handled in this "confederation of entrepreneurs" way.

WORKERS' PARTICIPATION?

That would provide more freedom and excitement at work for those who want to become entrepreneurs. But it would be an integral part of any scheme for "confederations of entrepreneurs" that non-entrepreneurial people should also have a wider choice of job satisfactions open to them. This may be the only viable way of solving the problem that peoples in the rich countries (who will generally be the most educated, and therefore include many of the most potentially productive) are going to become weary of working hard to grow richer long before people earning $200 a year do.

In rich societies, such as America has become, the decision whether any worker wants to get off the growth escalator should be an entirely personal one for him; but he should not be allowed to slow the whole escalator for the rest of mankind. Rich countries need to redesign their business systems so that each individual can decide whether to take his own share of the next decade's potential doubling of gnp per head in another doubling of his accumulated stock of material goods or in an extra six months holiday a year. Then while I go fishing most of you will fortunately choose to go on frenetically redoubling gwp like now.

The first step should be for workers to be able to state the job satisfactions they seek. Maybe Smith just wants $12,000 a year made with the smallest attendance at

37

work at dates chosen by him. Maybe Miss Jones wants to work under a father figure. Maybe Mrs Buggins wants a gossip at work (put her on a Swedish circular production line?). Maybe Browne wants to be a lazy genius, and Braun to be a frenetic one. Maybe total flexitime is important to some people, and total orderliness to others.

Computerised job data banks must eventually be set up withing big companies, so that the job-wants expressed can be matched to the job-offers provided by corporations, through a flexible market system. If a huge number of people said they wanted six months off each year (which I would not expect), then the wage attractable by the few who were ready to stick to their job year-round would go up proportionately and that attractable by the long-vacationists would go down (which would both influence firms to change their working habits so as to be able to use the bargain long-vacationists and also make long-vacationing suddenly less popular). If a large number of people showed they wanted to be entrepreneurs (which I think is very likely), then the performance contracts offered would become meaner, but, the vanity of entrepreneurs being greater than the eagerness of those going on six months' holiday with the wife, I think we would still get a lot of entrepreneurs at that bargain price—and some would succeed, which is exactly what we need in a world where there are too few entrepreneurs on offer at present.

The more one mulls over this broad idea, the more it makes sense that rich countries will have to move towards something like it. It is plain that free people in in-dustrial countries need to be given a greater say in what they choose as their conditions of work. This will either have to be consumer freedom, or producer democracy.

Consumer freedom is what you have when you can buy your groceries at several competing supermarkets; we need to be able to choose our lifestyles with at least as much freedom as we choose our brands of soap (and our choice between soaps is now wide and good). Pro-ducer democracy means you choose by voting who will run your workplace, just when electorates all over the world are finding that voting for Nixon-Agnew or McGovern-and-originally-Eagleton is no good way of

Post 1776 take-off

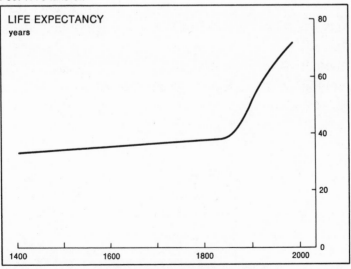

Reprinted with permission of Macmillan Publishing Co., Inc., from *World Facts and Trends*, Second Edition, by John McHale. © copyright 1972 by John McHale.

39

choosing who should run a whelkstall. Producer democracy would also put more power into the hands of trade unions. Although trade unions all over the world are telling governments that this is what the people insistently demand, yet people all over the world are showing in public opinion polls that they want precisely the opposite.

In Europe the power of trade unions is already so large that they may force unsuccessful experiments in producer democracy. In America the power of trade unions is smaller (sometimes because unions are more sensible, sometimes because they are more criminal); and my guess is that there is a greater hope that American corporations may move towards becoming confederations of entrepreneurs and showplaces of consumer freedom. But American businesses have not considered this yet.

American society has not considered the even more exciting 200th birthday possibilities lying ahead of it either.

AGENDA
FOR
WORLD
LEADER

No problems for the future: energy, food, minerals. Real problems: living too long, and . . .

On the first day of our Lord, when the order had gone out from Caesar Augustus that all the world should be counted, there were probably around 250m human beings (15), with an average annual income per head of $100 in terms of today's money. On the first day of the United States, on July 4th of 1776, there were probably around 700m human beings, with the same average annual income per head. The world then stood at one minute to dawn after 10,000 years of technological stagnation.

The average Roman citizen in AD 1 seems to have had a slightly higher annual income (guessed at today's equivalent of just under $300 a head) than his successor citizen 1775 years later in the next great republic (just under $200 a head for the United States in 1776). The man of 1776 used much the same energy sources as the man of AD 1 (animal muscle, wind and water); he could travel much the same tiny maximum distance per day; he used much the same materials for tools (wood and iron) and had much the same average expectation of life (to his late 30s or early 40s), although Rome's standards of big-city sanitation were better. Rome reached a population of a million, which no subsequent city dared to do until London after 1800, because the million-people-megalopolis did not seem safe under post-Roman but pre-1800 standards of cleanliness, plague control, law and order protection, and unmechanised transport of

Post 1776 take-off

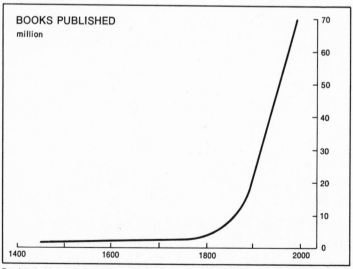

Reprinted with permission of Macmillan Publishing Co., Inc., from *World Facts and Trends,* Second Edition, by John McHale. © copyright 1972 by John McHale.

peasant or feudal agriculture's products into the towns. The two really big technological advances between AD 1 and 1776 were in killing power (gunpowder by 1776 had several times the killing area of arrows) and information technology (Gutenberg's printing press after 1441 increased the circulation potential of each written word several hundredfold).

Then, shortly after 1776, all the charts scattered through this survey took off with a whoosh.

Between 1776–1975 world population has increased sixfold, real gwp eightyfold, the distance a man can travel a day between a hundredfold and a thousandfold, the killing area of the most effective megadeath weapon over a millionfold, the amount of energy that can be released from a pound of matter over 50 millionfold (with much more to come) and the range and volume of information technology several billionfold (although how do you compare the range of an orator's voice in 1776 with Neil Armstrong's telecast from the moon to everybody's drawing room, or an abacus with a computer?).

GROWTH TO COME

Note that the things which cause gwp to increase (potential energy, information technology, etc) have already increased by thousands or even millions of times more than gwp itself, so that there is a lot of existing technology still to work through to living standards as well as even more new technology to come. In 1975, when it is fashionable to forecast that world growth is about to stop, technological realism suggests that growth is more probably at an early stage of an extraordinary acceleration.

The eightyfold increase in real gwp since 1776 has been based on man's increase in control over matter and energy, at a pace that has risen in each of the last 20 decades after having stood still in the previous 10,000 years. To this matter-cum-energy-revolution there has been added in the past two decades a breakthrough in the processing of information (computers, etc) and a nascent breakthrough in the distribution of information (telecommunications by satellite, the beginnings of packaged and computerised "learning programmes", maybe even at last a start towards understanding of the learning process itself).

During 1950–73 real gwp was increasing at an annual average 5%, which meant that it doubled about every 14 years. It will be surprising if during most of America's third century 1976–2076 the world does not have the potential to grow considerably more quickly than that. But note, first, that even if only 5% annual growth were continued, then by 2045 today's $5½ trillion gwp would be over $175 trillion and by 2059 it would be over $350 trillion. My guess is that by 2059 world population might be around 15 billion, and people probably would not want a gwp much higher than that trebling for every human of America's present gnp per head. Note, second, from Table 1 the distribution of income with which the world starts. Two-thirds of mankind are still living at pre-1776 levels of under $300 a head. The other third of us have average incomes between five and 25 times as high. Trillion in this survey means, in the American language, one million million; and billion means a thousand million.

There is a temptation to preach to any world leader

TABLE 1: GROSS WORLD PRODUCT

	Population (million)	Total gnp ($ billion)	Gnp per head ($)	Annual gnp growth 1960–73 (%)
United States	215	1,500	7,000	4
Other industrial (west Europe, Japan etc)	550	2,300	From 3,300 (Britain) to 7,000	From 3 (Britain) to over 10
"Middle class" (communist Europe, Mediterranean, some fast developers)	550	850	1,550	5 to 10
Oil countries	150	200	From 300 (Nigeria) to over 10,000	Erratic
Poor countries	2,550	650	250	Generally around 5
Total	4,000	5,500	1,400	Around 5

from Table 1 on the way in which he should determine to help distribute these many chickens for every pot. But what may stop them from being hatched?

American ecologists—who for some reason think that all the post-1776 charts which have risen with a whoosh will now drop with a whoosh—say growth is going to be stopped by a shortage of energy, food and raw materials (especially metals) plus high pollution and high birth rates. These seem, in fact, the five least likely forecasts for the next 20 years. Instead, the three biggest worries over the next three decades may be: a fall in the old people's death rate, a growth in mass-killing-power, and the danger that new knowledge will expand out of control. But consider the five red herrings first.

TOO MUCH ENERGY, NO POLLUTION

There are many thousand possible ways of releasing energy from storage in matter (16). They range from petty ways, like 25 BTUs per pound of matter by letting a pound of elastic bands untwist; through fairly petty ways, like 20,000 BTUs by burning a pound of petrol; through more sophisticated ways like 250m BTUs from the fission of the U-235 isotope in one pound of natural uranium; up to 260 thousand billion BTUs from the fusion to helium of a pound of hydrogen. Note that this last system, in which the waters of the oceans could serve as a limitless reservoir of fuel, would be over 10,000,000,000 times more effective per pound of matter than burning a pound of the Arabs' oil.

The trend since 1776 has been for new technology to drive on in sudden bursts towards the cleaner power sources nearer the top of the range. The present "energy crisis"—ie, the raising to 100 times its marginal cost of the asking-price for the inconvenient mineral slime that is temporarily considered the most transportable energy source—must make the next burst a bit faster. The likely speed of the coming glut in oil might best be gauged by the speed with which other sources were displaced when oil became cost-effective (oh, those poor interwar coalminers and horses), by the range of known future alternatives (unprecedented, including fusion, solar, geothermal, ocean-gradient, renewable-cellulose-into-clean-alcohol, a lot of others) and by the inefficiency with which all industrial countries have used fossil fuels (generation, storage and transmission mechanisms have long been archaic).

A big advantage is that each new energy source tends to be much less pollutant than the last one. A horse (17) dragging a cart through an urban mile emits 600 grams of solid pollutant and 300 grams of liquid pollutant; a motor car emits only 6 grams of pollutant of any sort; a battery-driven car will emit . . . ? Pittsburgh and London peasoup fogs have largely disappeared with soft King Coal.

THE COMING GLUT OF FOOD

The present world political system is that nearly all poor countries (under an annual $500 a head) rig their economic policies against their farmers—and then find that the universally-high elasticity of supply in agriculture means that their countries are very short of food; while nearly all rich countries (over $1,000 a head) rig their economic policies in favour of their farmers—and then find that the universally-high elasticity of supply in agriculture saddles them with butter mountains. Over the next three decades most countries will move above the $1,000 a head mark, and we will suddenly find ourselves swimming in food gluts.

Shortages in food supply per head of local population are not nowadays well correlated with soil conditions. India-Pakistan-Bangladesh, the most tragic area, has more arable land than the United States, great ability for multiple cropping, a more bountiful water supply. (18) More interestingly, the elasticity of food supply (ie, the usual % rise in supply in response to a % rise in real price) is not nowadays well correlated with social conditions.

In the five years after 1965 there were huge increases in wheat and rice yields in India-Pakistan (aided by the politicians' temporary emphasis on agriculture, by favourable terms of trade for petroleum-based fertilisers, by the green revolution, maybe by good weather), so that India temporarily became self-sufficient in agriculture. If these increases in yields had been continued for a century, the world would have been destroyed because its entire surface would have been covered by rice to a depth of three feet (19). But then Indian and Pakistani politicians turned to concentrate their budgets on more bellicose things, and higher energy prices moved the terms of trade against the farmers.

Agriculture in the rich countries is now uneconomically energy-intensive, so it is easy for those who count in megajoules to say there is wild exaggeration in the argument that if all the land now cultivated were brought up to Dutch standards of efficiency, then the world could feed 60 billion people, 15 times today's population. Instead, there is understatement. This estimate refers only to the tiny 3% of the globe's surface that is now farmed. It ignores the fact that in most poor countries there has not been a serious "green revolution" study of the best methods and crops. It underestimates the fact that 70% of crops in some poor parts of the world are eaten by easily-destroyable pests. It takes no account of the way plant growths can already be increased between tenfold and a hundredfold in plastic greenhouses or other scientifically controlled chambers free of diseases and pests. And the chemical equivalent of outdoor protection by plastic greenhouses is bound to come.

Above all, it ignores the waste in the present extraordinary agricultural system of turning grain into meat through very inefficient livestock converters (20).

The world's pigs today eat seven times more primary protein than the world's North Americans. The world's horses (now often a recreational animal) eat more than its Chinese. The world's cows (a third of them Afro-Asian non-producers) eat more grain than all the world's people. With apologies to cows, our children will move to rearing food by conversion of cellulose by enzymes and of petroleum wastes by single-cell high-protein organisms. Listen to America's J. Leon Potter:

> A *pound of bacteria, feeding on crude oil so worthless that it is burned as waste, can grow fast enough to produce 10 pounds of protein in a day. If a yearling calf were able to manufacture protein at the same rate, it would end the day roughly the size of a three-car garage and it would have consumed several tons of expensive grain in the process. The cost of protein produced from waste effluents is approaching 3 cents/pounds, compared with agriculture and animal protein at 10 cents/pound. Algae produces protein at a rate of 30 to 50 tons/acre/year, compared with the conventional agriculture of 3 to 5/tons/acre/year. (21)*

Will this food from bugs be made palatable? Unfortunately, yes. It is already possible to make sewage taste like stew.

The real food problem for the future is rich men's

habit of eating more food than is good for health, partly because of the accident that "entertaining", both social and business, has morbifically become attached to this natural function, rather than to the two that are assumed to be more disgusting than a drunken guzzle (defecation and sex), or than to the civilised Roman one. It will be wise in this next century to go back to holding social gatherings and informal business negotiations in what could now be various exciting sorts of baths.

ON YOUR METALS

Five of the world's 16 main metals are in virtually limitless supply (iron, aluminium, magnesium, titanium, silicon) (22). Four others are subject to continuing improvements in the mining process, and the next will be the big step of just picking up nodules from the ocean floor (copper, cobalt, manganese, nickel). That leaves seven whose long-term prices might rise sharply if today's "known reserves" were the most economic way of mining them (chromium, lead, zinc, tin, gold, silver, mercury). But the whole anti-intellectual concept of talking about "known reserves" of anything, including oil, is often the last refuge of the scoundrelly oil company's public relations officer. Listen instead to Professor Wilfred Beckerman:·

51

Given the natural concentrations of the key metals in the earth's crust, as indicated by a large number of random samples, the total natural occurrence of most metals in the top mile of the earth's crust has been estimated to be about a million times as great as present known reserves. Since the latter amount to about a hundred years' supplies this means we have enough to last about one hundred million years. Even though it may be impossible at present to mine to a depth of one mile at every point in the earth's crust, by the time we reach the year AD *100,000,000 I am sure we will think up something.* (23)

Other rather obvious points: the world does not actually consume metals at all, but employs them in ways that make them available for re-use after anything between 3 and 25 years (ie "known reserves" should include all the already used metals eventually available for recycling) (24); most of the industrial materials used today were not even conceptually recognised a short time ago, and most of the materials that will be used in the coming century are not conceptually recognised today; substitutions through plastics, etc, will hugely increase; and micro-miniaturisation with integrated circuits means that it is going to be increasingly economic to put on to a chip the size of a postage stamp properly connected electrical circuits which would previously have required assemblies of machinery that fill a room.

One mineral probably is going to be short for a while,

because countries have foolishly made it a free good: water.

POPULATION: THE FIRST WORRY

At last year's World Population Conference in Bucharest, the United Nations Secretariat presented a World Plan for Action (on which it had been working for years), calling for a reduction of world population growth to 1.7% a year by 1985. Nobody liked to point out that world population growth had probably fallen to 1.7% a year already. (25)

The anti-baby hysteria of the 1960s was a classic of trendy innumeracy. It came after a fall in fertility rates had been made certain by the breakthrough in both birth control technology (the pill, etc) and in birth control attitudes (acceptance of abortion and of papal fallibility). By 1972 the World Bank was already reporting a decline in fertility in 56 of the 66 countries for which meaningful data on births are available (26); but those whose jobs depended on the continued organisation of the anti-baby World Population Year pressed on regardless. The result will now be a risk of emotion the other way. It is already fashionable to say that the present 4 billion world population will still be under 6 billion by the year 2000. This is probably wrong, because the next problem has not been foreseen.

Awkwardly, medicine is bound eventually to make a breakthrough in curing the main degenerative diseases, so that old people will start to exist longer. This will set the real population problem. As the death rate drops, mankind will probably have to move towards acceptance of euthanasia and even planned death (with a hell of a going-away party on your 85th birthday?). (27)

My guess is that mankind will accept this smoothly. Witness how abortion was a word you could not mention to auntie 15 years ago, but today any woman could get an abortion in most cities by next weekend. It will not be at all surprising if there is in some quite near decade-and-a-half a similarly swift and equally civilised dash to acceptance of killing off old codgers (by then, like me) as there has been, in so short a twinkling, towards the more emotive act of killing unborn babies. Acceptance of planned death means that mankind must then surely alter all the lifestyles for all the ages of present individual existence as well.

But this had better be discussed later, after first pondering whether the real dangers of 1976–2076 will allow mankind lifestyles at all.

BOMBS
FOR
EVERYBODY?

Real needs: a plan for gwp, and a recognition that control over killing power will become dangerously more difficult, while control over people's brains will become dangerously (?) easier.

One thermonuclear warhead can now release more energy than all the gunpowder and TNT exploded in all the wars of history (28). So far nuclear weapons have been in the hands only of countries mature enough not to want to blow their neighbours up. But a raw young Massachusetts postgraduate student showed last year that anybody can now work out from published material how to make atomic bombs. All countries and some criminals will eventually be able to knit their own.

The leaders of more than half the world's 150 governments nowadays go to bed each night knowing that they might conceivably be executed after a violent coup d'état tomorrow. This does not make for a calm and unexcitable mind in the lower half of what will be the nuclear-trigger-minders' profession. Within recent memory only one black civilian African government has democratically handed power to an opposition after an election; that was Somalia, now a military dictatorship like the rest.

It is clear that the world's rich north must devise a new policy towards its poor south, and that the policy cannot be that of keeping troops in all poor countries to stop them blowing the world up (ie, cannot be colonialist). It had therefore better be economic, aimed at maximisation of gwp, and America had better set the pace. Some will say that maximisation of gwp will be pollutant (at a time when nine out of ten humans still lack sanitary disposal?) and disruptive (in a world where most of those on annual incomes under $200 are black or brown?). These stagnationists will also quote more and more black and brown dictators on their side.

The dictators who rule most poor countries may increasingly not want industrial development because their main interest, understandably, is to delay the day when they will be murdered during their successor's coup d'état. Industrialisation adds two new classes (an internationalised merchant class, an urban working class) to the two (the army and the political colleagues) who organise these 3 AM revolutions. The dictators of today's poor countries can best be regarded as like the monarchs of pre-industrial Europe, but dependent for succession on palace revolutions instead of on the (for pre-industrial countries) more convenient because more peaceful absurdity of primogeniture. American liberals would be unwise to suppose that many of these present dictators will be as progressive as the monarch under whom leadership of world economic advance began, George III.

PLAN FOR GWP

Nevertheless, the right geo-political-economic target for the next 30 years is definable. It should be to repeat what has luckily happened with Russia in the last 30 years. The Russians had an Idi-Amin-type leader in Stalin in 1945, and it then seemed rather likely that they would blow up the world. They now probably will not do so because there is a broad enough stratum of people in or near the decision-taking cadres in Russia who have a tolerably pleasant life, and do not intend to allow Mr Brezhnev or any immediate successor to incinerate it. As nuclear plants will proliferate, it will be advisable similarly to embourgeois the bottom half of the world in a devil of a hurry.

The best mechanism would be something like this. At present nearly all big industrial countries look forward to what their gnps may be a year ahead, and pump in extra spending power if there looks like being underdemand.

The rich countries should start instead to look forward to what gwp may be a year ahead, and must often pump any desirable extra spending power initially into the hands of the poorer countries (extra SDRs created so they can expand their imports?). Their use of this would then mop up unwanted unemployment in the world's rich north.

The objective should be to raise ever more countries to the sort of income level where their governments will be composed of people who think of themselves and their political opponents as heading slowly towards comfortable retirement, instead of racing to get their brothers-in-law to the firing squad first. Probably the best definition of the sort of government that will not start nuclear fighting is: any government where the decision-makers assume that they personally will end their lives in the local equivalent of Southern California, a dacha outside Moscow, or the House of Lords. This seems usual at gnps per head over about $1,000 a year.

CRIME PREVENTION

The uppermost thought of members of the Baader-Meinhof or Manson gangs, of teenage paranoiacs and of professional kidnappers is not that they are likely to end their years in the House of Lords. But both mass-killing-power and more selective-killing-power are going to come into their sorts of hands.

Some time there is likely to be a demand from some small organisation that society do something intolerable or else a megadeath weapon will be exploded in some big American city or hurled in on the next world summit meeting. Organised crime will increase its present rather low technological efficiency. Murder from a distance will become much easier—such as by telephoning a victim from anywhere and exploding down the wire a device loud enough to shatter his eardrum.

There will have to be redefinition of the objectives of criminal justice, in ways that may look gruesome. Just as one frightening technology is bringing the world to a stage where some criminals will have an explosive power a million times greater than strong lunatics have ever had before, another frightening technology is going to make it possible to control their brains and minds and moods. Electrodes planted in the brain—and eventually able to switch themselves on and off—are going to be able to control irrational aggression; while love-inducing, placidity-inducing, apathy-inducing mood pills are going to multiply by the million. It is almost certain that governments will use these, on the grounds that "some crimes are diseases which can best be treated by drug therapy."

Outpatient treatment for those with records of violence may involve a great loss of privacy. Data on felons

will be readily available for tracing the most likely criminal when there has been a mugging in Central Park
with a left-hand downward blow at an angle of 77°, and
for suggesting the right medicament for him. Police cars
hurrying to an incident will have direct access to these
computerised data banks. TV cameras already watch
some high crime streets in America; this will be extended. Some clients of the probation and parole services (which will be merged) will have to carry electronic identifying instruments around with them so that
there can be checks on where they are. Frighteningly,
tests have shown that even closely-watched laboratory
rats become perturbed (and more deviant) with loss of
privacy; but these will be outpatients who might blow up
the world.

It has become fashionable (chiefly because of
America's own protests and determination to clip its
CIA) to portray the organisations and institutions of the
United States as unfitted to handle these horrible social
innovations that are likely to be forced on mankind. My
own view, as will become apparent through the rest of
this survey, is that America will have a better chance of
lighting the way forward, while keeping going the vital
continuing debate on civil liberties, than anyone else.
American government does keep open most of the possible routes of appeal, in Byron's phrase, from tyranny to
God.

AGES OF MAN

America may also have the best chance of tackling the next big problem, because its experience of the problem is most advanced. It has become clear that there is something dreadfully wrong with the handling of the present four ages of man: childhood, adolescence, rat race and retirement.

Citizens of most countries spend the first and most formative 15 years of their lives under the haphazard control of untrained parents, in a grim lottery according to whether they have drawn a parent who rears a delinquent or a paranoid or an integrated human being.

The first of two new horrors lately added through good intentions is that medical advances have pushed the opening age of rebellious adolescence down well below 15, while governments have been pushing the age to which such kids must be kept behind small desks above 15. The second is that for the next age-group— from 15–25—the rich countries under American leadership have made a noble and massive and plainly disastrous experiment during this last half of the American century, during 1925–1975.

At the beginning of the half-century, the great majority of the 15–25 age group were in paid work. Now very many in America and its imitators are in school on state-aided funds even after the age of 18. In an era when the social sciences are an exploding growth recrea-

61

tion, one might expect the last three decades' observed results of this experiment to be constantly re-assessed. They are not assessed, because they are sociologically inconvenient.

The observed results in most rich countries are a huge rise in the crime rate in the 12–24 age group (which now commits most of all industrial countries' most worrying crimes), a devastating impact on family relationships especially among the urban poor and the suburban rich, an increased difficulty in handling the problems of puberty and adolescence, a flight by teenagers to pot, and the assumption by employers that anybody who leaves education beore 23 belongs to the dimmer half of society (so that American business is being reorganised to ensure that full-time jobs for under-23s dry up). When efforts are made to counter this by pushing still more of the rejected minority (especially black minority) into college, this (a) causes the now-slightly-smaller but still large minority left out to be regarded as still-more-obviously-unemployable, and (b) breeds a catastrophic failure rate among the new undergraduates, so that they congregate in separate groups which defy integration while inferiority complexes among them mount.

In the third age of man, after age 24, males (and some women) have 40 years of climbing up the seesaw of a career, usually having least time to spend with their children just when they should be doing most to bring them up. Then at the age of 65 they are suddenly stripped of all status—and, in an inflationary age, of a large part of their spending power—until they die 10 or 15 years later, although with the unpleasant prospect that this period may soon be incontinently extended. When it is extended, I suspect that mankind will be right to accept a system of planned death.

A main task for the early years of the 1976–2076 century will be radically to reshape these wrong ages for human lifestyles. There is no possibility that the right new shape will be decided by the liberal central governments of major powers. Their efforts so far have greatly worsened the mess. The best hopes will lie in experiments by competing governments, or competing communities, within some great society. And that is another reason why it will be a pity if world leadership passes from America in present mid-torrent.

THE
DREAMY
MONSTER

*America has the right government sys-
tem for running a free enterprise society;
but the wrong one for running the one-
third socialist society into which it has
meandered*

There are three key points about the way in which the
Americans rule themselves, but many Americans have
not yet recognised the last two. To begin with the old
hat:

(1) The American system is to set up lots of competing governments—both at Washington (as between executive and supreme court and congress and all those
task forces and a shifting establishment) and at local
level (where the overlapping between the thousands of
local authorities is now being compounded by greater
overlapping within themselves as they also proliferate
advisory committees, etc). This system has one huge advantage. As Madison saw when he created it, multigovernment saves America from being ruled by a "tyr-

annous majority". It also has several interesting side-effects, and now one huge but correctable disadvantage.

(2) The disadvantage is that this dreamy monster of American multigovernment is the most inefficient body for spending money on non-specific and non-measured objectives that could be conceived. As it now has more money (about $½ trillion) to spend annually on non-specific and non-measured objectives than the entire annual income of the poorest half of people in the world, this is awkward.

Any Cassandra would have been accused of making a mortally-sick joke if she had forecast what would happen in the past quarter-century after the two greatest surges in public expenditure in world history. After America's "defence shift" (29) (ie, the diversion to defence between 1948 and the mid-1950s of 9% of America's huge and growing gnp), the military establishment thus expensively created managed to lose an unnecessary war to slightly ridiculous North Vietnam. Then after the "welfare shift" (ie, the diversion between 1960 and the early 1970s of another 9% of America's huge gnp to help, in particular, the urban poor) life for the urban poor became unmitigated hell. Crime in their home areas soared, family structures were destroyed, education and other public services rotted, cheery if dirty inner cities became neurotic and dirtier inner cities. At a cost in social welfare expenditure that rose from $24 billion in

1950 to $242 billion in 1974 America sprouted a welfare system that more often crippled than aided its clients and their neighbours.

(3) The Americans are likely to react to this failure of managerial government either mainly in one silly way or mainly in one sensible way. The silly way (at present being widely urged) is to "increase participation": ie, to set up ever more competing units of governments so that all the 5% of people who are interested in government as a hobby can eventually join some local coordinating committees to be coordinated by other coordinators. This would further strengthen America's admirable and already inviolable defences against being ruled by a tyrannous majority, but it would also mean that the volume and inefficiency of government spending of money would grow and grow.

The sensible reform is to reorganise the system in favour of the 95% of people who are interested in governments as consumers of their services, not as would-be participatory producers of them. This (see below) should involve the transfer from bureaucratic to marketplace mechanisms of many of today's public services. A great deal for the world will depend on which of these two roads America takes. But consider the other two points first.

SO MANY GOVERNMENTS

The first consequence of America's possession of so many competing units of government is that a marvellously radical range of proposals for every issue is very quickly mooted, but a rather conservative range of proposals is then rather slowly put into effect (30). Action on any proposals will impinge on perhaps 20 bodies' bailiwicks, so the eventual decision-maker usually blocks ideas that could be called kooky, both in order to avoid giving offence to the perhaps 10 conservative agencies in his multifold consensus and to avoid giving the encouragement of precedent for their own odd suggestions to his perhaps nine other kooks. The exception is when this long delay in bringing any decision causes (or is deemed to have caused) a crisis. Then the American system is that all the ideas, both the conservatives' and the kooks', are adopted in a bunch. This is how there came about all the three big surges (the "new deal" shift of the 1930s, the "defence shift" of the 1950s, the "welfare shift" of the 1960s), which carried America's peacetime government spending from 11% of gnp in 1929 to today's 33%—in three rushes, and by mistake.

As I believe that domestic decisions made by governments since the war have usually done slightly more harm than no decisions would have done, I did not consider until this trip that the usual delay of decision-making through the multigovernment system had done America any net damage in non-crisis years. But during this trip I began to believe that America's multigovernment system had sprouted, even for non-crisis years, some new disadvantages.

First, it must be a disadvantage that the last two elected Presidents of the United States have been driven paranoid as they sat like spiders at the centre of this multifold web of argumentative and often cleverer people, and felt that they and their own Haldemans or Rostows were beleaguered in a world of traducing enemies from the bureaucracy and establishment and media. My guess is that Humphrey and McGovern are the type who would also have been upset by this. Could it have led them, too, to suppose that bugging and deception and worse were part of the necessary process of government, as both Johnson and Nixon did?

President Ford does not feel paranoid at being regarded as a "footballer who played too long with his helmet off", because he has good-naturedly been accustomed to that sort of taunt all his life. But something does seem wrong with an election process when the last presidential election was won with the largest majority in America's 200 years of history by two men who were at that moment chargeable as accomplices of different felons, and when the next election seems liable to be won with a large majority by a president who was elevated by the multifold consensus to the top job in the world largely because the opposing party wrongly thought him too dumb to offer it a threat in 1976.

The great hope is that the American people may be showing much more sense than the participators in political caucuses. Except for John Kennedy the worst sorts of honest men to be American President have probably been those who have been regularly nominated by the main parties since 1960. The voters may now have woken to this. Last year the Democratic party leaders did not endorse Hugh Carey for governor of New York because he could not win, and he then won because they did not endorse him (31). To a cool decision-maker, with all those ingenious alternative ideas coming in from all those competing sources, the job of President of the United States could now be enormously productive fun—provided only that all parts of American government could get new controls on spending.

THE $500 BILLION QUESTION

America's multi-consensus Madisonian system is now causing the money spent on government to soar and yet be insufficient at the same time. When one body in government gets money for a programme, another body that has been fighting against it has to be given some money for another programme, but economies are usually sought by ensuring that the share available to each is insufficient to carry its particular programme through. Moreover, competition rarely extends to the point where one government body assesses the inefficiency of its rival's achievements, because it is afraid of counter-assessment back. The reliance on Congress for this won't work.

While European democracies were built downward by the gradual forced extension of aristocrats' noblesse oblige, American democracy was built upwards by the elevation into at least a twentieth-century advertising agency's ethics of nineteenth-century precinct-politicians like Boss Tweed. The founding fathers had spotted the danger, which is why they gave America a constitution for governments with few powers and those mostly negative. This and the Boss Tweed tradition are awkward for multigovernments spending $500 billion a year.

The politician's art in America is that of successful negotiation among proliferating organisations, whom he usually promises he will try to get more money for. He often shocks an innocent European by publicly favouring government expenditure for which he admits in private that intellectually there is no case ("politically important to me"). The old tradition of safeguarding the taxpayer's dollar has faded in areas where over a fifth of a politician's wage-earning constituents are often paid by that dollar, where his local big business constituents depend on contracts from it, and where his welfare-drawing constituents make up another large group.

In parts of local government all this has created what Americans call "New York's British disease".

LITTLE BRITAIN IN NEW YORK

"Welcome to your own country" (or something rudely similar), said three of the four prominent New York intellectuals whom I started to question on their city's plight. The pattern is uncosily familiar.

First, rent control predictably destroyed New York's housing market. Then the flight of the property-tax-paying white middle classes to federally-guaranteed or GI Joe mortgages in the suburbs brought their replacement in their now-rotting New York tenements by poor blacks and dark Hispanics. They helped to frighten some New York businesses away. Then the City of New York started during the "welfare shift" to spend on public sector activities a British-style proportion of the gross metropolitan product which the property-taxpayers' flight now made it impossible for it to collect. The first results of this "welfare shift" were that control over New York passed into the hands of the public-sector-trade-unions, who were able to crucify the city with huge pension-

and-pay rises and impossibly low productivity. The Americans carry this to extremes. As witness:

● After twenty years' service New York city employees can and do move to another job, carrying an unconditional (and periodically-raised) lifetime pension based on their final year's earnings. Results, in a country where most males work for over 40 years: the city is effectively becoming committed to paying for two labour forces of 350,000 people each; in his twentieth year every subway worker puts in a lot of overtime.

● Private enterprise carters in New York can make a profit collecting garbage if paid one-third the costs per ton that city garbage collectors show.

● Expenditure per pupil in New York City's schools was around $2,250 last year (not much less than total personal disposable income per head in Britain), while in church-affiliated schools in the Archdiocese of New York it was only about one-quarter of that. Reading standards in New York's city schools are lower than in diocesan schools.

● The mayor of New York told a conference this year that his bankrupt city has 160,000 employees working for social welfare programmes such as income maintenance, food stamps, medical and housing assistance. Since most welfare workers get salaries above the national average, and since the main observable statistical effect of welfare programmes in New York City has been to increase the number of social workers there, it may, says one American scholar, "be hypothesised that most spending on social programmes designed to eliminate poverty in fact increases income inequality" in New York. (32)

PERFORMANCE CONTRACTS

The economic reasons are now overwhelming for America to lead the capitalist world to total overhaul of its grossly inefficient system of public-sector spending. The logical solution must lie with subjecting more of that $500 billion a year now deployed by American politicians and bureaucrats to various sorts of competition through market mechanisms. Eventually, to quote John Diebold again (33), the output of every unit in the public sector will have to be assessed (eg, objective measures of "are the streets cleaner?") Then if anybody tenders on a performance contract that it could provide greater output at less cost, the citizens should have a chance of engaging it on one of the many devisable systems which would ensure that this particular entrepreneur would have the finance to expand further only if he did improve performance.

The Americans pick the purveyors of the less essential two-thirds of their services and goods (like soapsuds) by competitive consumer choice, and the purveyors of the more essential one-third (like street-lighting) by casting political ballots. At present the mechanism for picking purveyors of soapsuds (free market competition plus mendacious advertising plus independent assessments by consumers' associations) is plainly working better than the mechanism (known as the great democratic process) for picking President Nixons and Mayor Beames. This is not a matter of personalities. Democratic elections are the best way of choosing whom we want to decide on great issues of peace and war, but not the best way of picking what is the best rapidly changing technology with which to run the drains.

The need is to extend voter participation in defining what the community wants from a public service, but then to extend new sorts of market competition to find who can most efficiently provide it. Probably the tele-communications and computer terminal revolution (see next article) will pave the way for this. It should be possible to use cable television for an "electronic town meeting" to discuss, with extensive use of all our computer terminals, the "production function" the citizens want from a public service. The production function chosen for a transport system might be: "ensure that there will be some transport mode by which people can get from the city centre to named suburbs in under 30 minutes at any time of the day". Then competing bids could come for this contract from private firms seeking performance contracts, from the municipal government, maybe from other towns' governments with relevant experience. One contractor might bid: "to fulfil my contract I must be allowed to charge private cars for passage over centre-city streets at times of congestion, but will offer the following car parks, pedestrian precincts, public transport modes." Then the people can choose by majority vote which contractor they want to hire, but with absolute freedom, if the performance contract is not fulfilled, to change to another contractor.

ENTRENCHING THE WRONG POWERS

The mechanisms for changing contractors would not now be difficult (witness changes in ITV contractors in Britain, and the growth of performance bonds in America). The big barriers in the way will be the bureaucrats and the participators.

The bureaucrats will be defending their jobs and freedom from being shown up. The participators—ie, those who think that services should not serve consumers, but instead their own urge for power—are America's disease.

"If you create wealth in America, it fructifies. If you create power groups, they usually go corrupt", I wrote in my 1969 survey in *The Economist* on America ("The Neurotic Trillionaire"). In 1968, President Johnson's "community action programmes," calling for the "maximum feasible participation" of residents in the poor black areas, had led to the election of community groups on the usual tiny participatory turnouts (0.7% in

Los Angeles, 2.4% in Boston, 2.7% in Philadelphia), some of which had turned intimidatory and more of which had turned corrupt; this policy had helped to subject black Americans to minority mob rule within their own communities.

In the universities, I described then how student "participation" by tiny strongarm groups on some campuses invited the most direct comparisons with the way that Hitler's brownshirts operated in the Weimar republic: except that these youths used harassment of elderly liberal or conservative academics as the means of excitement of their followers' thug instincts, where Hitler used Jews.

In 1975 participation is much gentler, but revealing fate was to give me on my first morning in America a seat in the stalls of another farce.

AN EXPERIENCE OF PARTICIPATION

The speakers at the opening plenary session of the World Future Society's second general assembly were six world-renowned scholars whom some of us had come across an ocean to hear. These six Americans were by origin, to judge from their patronyms, one Scotsman, one Irishman, one Frenchman, one Italian and two Jews. You can say, if you wish, that that sounds like the opening sentence in a long bad joke. What you cannot say, unless you are devoid of any sense of your own ridiculousness, is that it is evidence of racism.

Yet here soon was a bossy woman forcing her way to a microphone to call, with applause from a prepared claque, for direct action because the six included no women and no blacks. There, at the next session, was a lady announcing a "compromise" that a number of women and blacks should present research papers which they had not in fact prepared, and asking all who supported this to show their solidarity with her group's direct action by standing. There, to my amazement, was I as almost the only seated person in my section of the hall, while elderly scholars of international renown scrambled to their feet like startled rabbits. I recognised half a dozen from their name tabs, and made a point of asking them why. All said that this interruption was very great nonsense; some denied that they had stood in its support, others muttered it was best to mollify this sort of thing.

Changing my delegate's badge for a press one, I went later to the women's caucus that chose its speakers. Not at all like 1969's black power guns at Cornell. Earnest, insecure, upper class but quite likeable lady prigs, each showing great solidarity (admittedly, usually between her ears) by seeking for slight to her sex, but of course then taken over by the more usual sorts of "partici-pators".

At the next plenary session we had two special speakers. The showpiece was a very articulate, very pre-

pared, very left-wing lady who roused the risen claque
with well-rounded phrases like "profit cannot exist save
with some debit item on the social or environmental
register somewhere." I was not surprised to hear later
that she is on one of Washington's advisory committees
for technology assessment. She was followed by a nice
black lady (ah, such participation!) whose scholarly cal-
ibre fell rather below that of the international scholars
whom we had travelled far to hear (and whose research
papers had been truncated so we could hear her). We all
applauded her so as to cover our embarrassment. Then,
at lunch, we were addressed by Senator Edward Kennedy. He inserted in his speech a sentence of commen-
dation for the direct action of that morning's left-wing
lady. I did not clap.

FACING YESTERDAY'S FUTURE

This was fascinating and gentle fun to watch, but it is
also the seminar age's equivalent of bookburning.
America is shaming itself by supposing it is democratic
that scholarship should be intimidated by shoddy, pre-
cooked populism. Luckily, it will not thus shame itself
for long. This should be a last hangover from the fact
that both politicians and professors understandably ran
scared in the 1960s, when the postwar-baby-bulge was
passing through lusty teenagehood in the campuses and

ghettoes, and when even a participatory 2% of that lumpy age group looked frightening as it waved banners or sometimes guns.

But now those babies of 1946, who in 1969 were 23-year-old Berkeley postgraduate students holding their passing-out demos, are 29-year-old executives in the Bank of America, where their main participatory actions are demands that stock options should also be available to 29-year-old executives (yes, honestly, for this is a generation not afraid to ask what it wants)—while their younger sisters and brothers born in the mid-1950s try to crowd into the supposedly-safe-job-creating medical schools or law schools, in a mass that will make those anyway-labour-over-intensive occuptions deep pools of professional unemployment by the mid-1980s.

America is not now very good at preparing to confront the future with any thoughtfulness. It is better at setting up institutions to study what was thought to be the future in the past. About six years ago all its places of learning got a rush of research funds to study the problems of the cities, the dreaded drift towards megalopolis. All those professors' departments are now just about ready to pour forth their research.

Meanwhile, five years ago, the trek back to the small towns and rural places began.

TOMORROW
WE'RE
HICKS

Without most people noticing this, America's reruralisation has begun. Will it work?

It is fascinating how quickly the Americans managed to create a very decent new small-town lifestyle during a single rather difficult decade near the beginning of their second century of 1876–1976. In one decade they all seemed to be shooting each other at the OK Corral, and in the next Dwight Eisenhower was being born at Abilene. In one decade the per capita murder rate in the cow towns and mining settlements was between 10 and 20 times that in New York today, and in the next decade these were the towns of the bible belt. The building of a great civilisation in the new young world leader in those brief 10 or 15 years after the 1870s had several foundation stones. The homesteaders who won the west were buoyed that they were fighting a moral crusade (as they spiked the existing farmers' free-ranging cattle with

81

their barbed wire) because they were creating settled communities with their wives, the Madonnas of the plains (34). Madonna, incidentally, even by 1900 lived only an average 47 years and was in the childbearing stage for 18 of them (35); the many children became self-reliant because they had useful chores to do from toddlerhood; there was a successful tradition of prying neighbourliness as everybody in and around each church-going small community knew everybody else.

Then, in a single rather easy decade near the end of their 1876–1976 century, the Americans somehow managed to create a rather nasty new city and suburban lifestyle. In the 1960s rural blacks poured into the cities, and the white middle classes poured into the suburbs, unexpectedly making both more horrid. Perhaps it should have been foreseen that the blacks in the cities would be cowboys (not homesteaders), and were escaping from a cloying religious atmosphere in the south-land (not proudly marching into one). Once newly in the cities their family structures often broke down, because you could get more pay packets if fatherhood was peripatetic and if the family unit was based on the welfare mother. The kids have nothing useful to do as they are chained to small desks and small apartments in tough streets during exploding adolescence, and are often left on the scrapheap through teenagehood because of high unemployment for the young unskilled; they are anonymous outside their street gangs. It is more

surprising that the white families moving into the suburbs in affluent pursuit of happiness seem so often to
have failed to catch up with it. But it now looks as if the
Dad-as-commuter lifestyle is often not a successful tribal
system; it has bred the suburban drug culture in which
the school-child goes to pot, mother takes tranquillisers
and the working husband drinks.

Americans say their "urban crisis" was the temporary
result of the huge rural-to-urban migration after Hitler's
war. Emigration out of the rural or nonmetro areas
(nonmetro means, broadly, a county with no town of
over 50,000) was 500,000 a year in the 1950s, just
under 300,000 a year in the 1960s. Many Americans
castigate the planners and sociologists for foolishly not
recognising early what was happening then, while themselves being unaware of what is happening now.

Between 1970–1973, the latest years for which there
are data, there was a population rise in America's nonmetro (ie, rural) areas of just over 350,000 a year (36).
Without many people noticing it, the tide is already
flowing back from both suburbia and the cities. The
next crisis of lifestyles will be that of reruralisation.
Early in its third century America will have to create a
new ex-urban lifestyle, probably again very suddenly.
The crucial topic of discussion should be what it will
be. At present this is not widely discussed.

TOWARDS TELECOMMUTERDOM

There are two reasons why I think that America will now lead the world toward the end of the urban age, although I agree that that end may have several false starts.

First, telecommuting is coming. When production is properly automated even in service industries, probably 60% of American breadwinners will be brainworkers. A brainworker can much more easily dispatch his work than himself to the office. Eventually workers will telecommute from their homes, but meanwhile telecommuting from neighbourhood work centres will begin. These will be places which will utilise the broadband two-way channels (37) that are attached to cable TV and where you will buy season tickets to have contact at will by picturephone and telex with all the colleagues and computers with whom you work—to exchange instant written and spoken and visual messages with them. Businesses still do not understand how cheap the marginal cost of all this is going to be. Murray Turoff has calculated that in remote African villages today computer-conferencing-systems based on mini-computers could be made available for the price of a cheap truck (38).

Businesses also do not realise that productivity will rise most sharply in precisely the fields where for decades face-to-face contact has wrongly been supposed to be most important. Once people are used to it, computer-augmented confravision across continents will be a more sensible way of getting 20 people to make a decision than ordinary face-to-face meetings, because each individual with his terminal can ask questions from a computer and everybody can look jointly at a screen; because views can be entered on the printout at each person's own convenience instead of everybody having to speak hurriedly after somebody else has spoken; because a usual process will be to leave a printout and videotape for executives not at the conference to see, so they can enter their own views within a strict timetable before a final decision is taken; because votes and sometimes inputs can be anonymous, so that all options can be tabled without fears of offending superiors; and because there is a "whispering" capability all through computer conferences, which allows timely subgroup negotiations without other conferees being aware these are taking place. All these at the chairman's volition. Most businesses' filing systems will become very largely computerised. Data will be fed into the computers from on-going conferences, and can be drawn on by a man living anywhere. The dash to the "paperless office" will probably become a fetish in the 1980s. Most of the 80% of America's first class mail which consists of business items is likely to be sent digitally by 1900, so mail-carrying will go very bust.

By the early 1980s a computer terminal should be as cheap as a colour TV set. It will quickly rise to become the principal business tool, and in a later surge will become a household mass durable. Household demand for computer terminals may initially be as an entertainment device. There are thousands of possible computer games, including detective games where you will try to discover something hidden in a computer and battlefield games where the computer will referee as you play Napoleon and beat Wellington at Waterloo, or you can say to the computer "anybody for bridge or a discussion group on such-and-such a subject?," and you will find partners and play on your screen, with the computer shuffling the cards. But household computer terminals will soon have more serious roles.

LIVING BY THE SCREEN

Telecommunications will alter society's patterns more profoundly than the previous and smaller transport revolutions of the railway and automobile have done. In tomorrow's scattered communities there will be telemedicare via multiphasic screening, remote physiological monitoring, remote supervision of work by paramedics, computer-assisted diagnosis, your own health record in a data bank; health care will become an efficient information-intensive business, instead of a hit-and-miss, labour-intensive one.

Education will move along the same electronic, audiovisual, individualised road; if some fiend was inventing the worst milieu in which to teach an over-10-year-old, he would invent one of today's school classrooms. Shopping will involve intelligent use of widespread and competitive consumer information retrieval systems (a telecomputerised "Which?," a telecomputerised Sears Roebuck), and instant electronic banking in place of cash deals. The launching of new models of, say, an automobile will be easier because the firm on a distant continent will tele-advertise its model from prototype stage, and offer substantial discounts for orders placed immediately. Consumers who like the thing will push buttons on their computer terminals (thus automatically debiting their bank accounts post-datedly for the day of delivery a declining number of months hence); and that will be the figure for the first production run. This conquest of initial market uncertainty will make the smaller, imaginative businesses and "confederations of entrepreneurs" thrive. (39)

Although all types of American nonmetro areas have simultaneously started growing again since 1970 (except the very agricultural, the very military, or the very black), two types have grown most. First, the rich men's outer exurbia—eg, fishing villages filled on weekdays by fishermen and top bankers' wives, but on weekends also by the bankers themselves, because New York is too far for daddy to commute every day. Urban interests say this shows the nonmetro revival is just suburban super-sprawl, but telecommuting patterns will be found more feasible now that the rich live furthest out (provided the rich like their wives). The other big nonmetro growth has been that on coasts, lakes, reservoirs, hills (Upper Great Lakes, Sierra Nevada foothills). Many of these are recreation-based upper-middle-class retirement areas, including part-time job country now that more upper-middle-class people retire early (you can choose to retire from many federal jobs at 55) (40). But they are signs that America still has a surprising number of nice and fairly-empty places to live.

The second reason why I think that the age of increasing urbanisation is over is that much of today's city and suburban lifestyle is now yesterday's hokum. Psychologists say that people catching up with happiness most usually need (a) social support systems from family or friends; (b) some sense of individual achievement; (c) some material wellbeing. The American-led century of 1876–1976 has provided one-third of mankind with material wellbeing, plus a greater width and equality of opportunity for individual achievement than is generally admitted, but now with some breakdown in the mechanisms feeding family life and friendships. To quote James Ramey: "In America our entire system of laws, customs, attitudes and human service delivery systems are set up to support the monogamous nuclear family, as though all Americans lived in such a family. But most Americans don't." (41)

OLD ORDER CHANGETH

With both teenager and grandma being driven (by impulse or expulse) away from their own folk earlier, over 60% of Americans at the time of the 1970 census did not live in a nuclear family with earning dad and housekeeping mum and the kids; they were childless couples or post-childrearing couples or single people or lived in other sorts of household. Nearly one in four of American bridegrooms has been married before, so plural marriages (ie, consecutive polygamy) are more common in America than in many countries which permit polygamy (42). Among under 25s the old conventions are now rare (single-parent families are growing at three times the rate of two-parent families), and by the time today's 25-year-olds are 35, the 20–35 age group will be 57% of America's adult population.

About 43m Americans move home every year, yet political representation is tied to geographical districts. This skews political action absurdly in favour of the minority who do not move (politicians favour rent controls, environmental protection, political action for existing interests but oppose new investment). It unfortunately makes it seem natural to Americans to gear new political action to the groups to which they belong more closely than they do to home town, but which are also, like Europe's immature nineteenth century nationalisms, selfish and antagonistic and jingoist (the dear old corporation, professional associations, trade unions, black power or women's lib). Americans will need instead to gear their political organisations to a situation where they now have the advantages (and some of the problems) of being as free as the birds in the air.

Increasing wealth and technology allow the inhabitants of rich countries to do something totally new in human history: namely, to live according to individual choice instead of in groups. (43) They are therefore naturally throwing away a lot of the old tribal restraints, religious conventions, patterns of obedience to authority, the moods of obsequiousness that were necessary when they lived in groups.

And then, very awkwardly, people are finding that they can be happy only if they do live in groups. It is pointless to say (although devotees of one of the next trendy emotional spasms will say this) that society must therefore return to being ruled by the old conventions, religious restrictions, craven obedience to the convenience of the boss at work. Individuals will not accept these restrictions now they see that wealth and the birth-control pill and transport technology make them no longer necessary, and anyway it is cramping of individual freedom to suggest that they should. But the next 25 years will show whether America is going to lead the world to a totally new and exciting society. At this end of this survey let me suggest only briefly the signposts and dangers to watch on the way.

RULES OF COMMUNITY

The key requirement for civilisation is that every individual should be able to make a deliberate choice about which community he wants temporarily to join, with absolute freedom to move to search for variety and with much fuller information than now about the alternative lifestyles available. That will require lots of independent assessments in data banks about how happy people living in particular communities are.

As telecommunications will greatly increase mobility, it will probably be right to finance telecommunication facilities much as roads have been financed. Once satellites are tossed into space, the marginal costs of using them do not vary greatly with distance of message sent, so it should become as cheap to telecommute daily to your office in New York from Tahiti as from next door.

While it is fun for the like-minded, perhaps four times a year, to get together, to dress outrageously alike and play around a little (as at a pop festival or a white-tie dinner) (44), a few consecutive months of living only with the like-minded will usually become impossibly contentious except under the sort of strict discipline that is acceptable only to nature's nuns. That is why today's hippy or other artificial communities don't work. Most of their members are too like-mindedly earnest in searching for a lifestyle, while the other 99.9% of us don't think about what we want nearly enough.

On the whole, I therefore discount the fear that the new communities will turn into impossibly inbred cloisters of bankers in one village, fetish hippies in another— although dangers of bigger class-splits arise because the first telecommuters will be the affluent, who may therefore learn less about ordinary people than ever as they work in electronic isolation from the underprivileged. (45) I am less worried by the argument that, after television has stopped us from making friends in our leisure time, so telecommuter terminals will stop social interaction at the workplace, and that all mechanisms for making friends will therefore stop. Small communities are generally matier, friends at the local telecommuter work centre will replace friends at the office (thus usefully eroding single-corporation ties). Americans will use telecommuting to make distant telefriends with whom they will play telebridge (and the data banks of America's third century will voraciously feed this business of computafriend). One of the main reasons for movement into a particular community will be a choice of some particular friend-making leisure activity associated with it (whether golf or boating or music), but not too exclusively.

How far should the law allow (indeed, encourage) variations in moral restrictions from place to place? Early in America's second century of 1876–1976 there was an extraordinary attempt to impose upper-middle-class bourgeois morality on the lower classes in both

North Europe and North America (with quite unnecessary laws against prostitution, gambling, alcohol, etc).
Late in America's second century there has been an
even more extraordinary attempt to impose upper-
middle-class bourgeois immorality on the lower classes
(46). The dash to the permissive society has everywhere
been led by upper-middle-class liberals, and has everywhere had its most miserable results for lower-middle-
class conservatives and the poor. It is the latter who have
suffered most from the breakdown of old family structures and taboos, from the de facto toleration of group
violence, from the habit of regarding muggers and
rapists as socially deprived kids (which is an unattractive
theory if a gang of socially-deprived mugging rapists is
liable to come to live in your apartment block). The
hardhats have a right to resent the softheads here.

A free man of the future must have an individual
choice between various communities with sharply contrasting lifestyles. It has been an advantage for America
that the existence of separate states allows experiments
with differing laws, but state boundaries are an an-
achronism. Decisions about community lifestyles will
have to be made much lower. The result in America's
third century will probably be a choice between more
puritan towns and middle-of-the-road ex-urban telecommuter areas with an interesting range of customs (rang-
ing on the right to groups of citizens who will have
hired some small Dutch or Japanese multinational com-

pany to run their local government on a renewable performance contract, and on the left to the participatory or the hippy).

SHADOWS BEFORE

This range of choices will be important as the world moves (a) through the stage of psychedelic and mood-affecting drugs, to the point where electronic stimulation of the pleasure centres of the brain becomes a rather easy technology (ie, to a stage where the manufacture of something which seems to most people indistinguishable from happiness may become artificially-creatable without any hangover); and (b)—here is the horror—where genetic engineering "advances" far enough for us to be able to mould special characteristics into babies and to stimulate artificial intelligence in human beings.

If the leading country in the world is centrally-governed as these last push-throughs are gradually made, then its central decision about them is likely to be either too restrictive or too permissive-by-default. If it is too restrictive, grey markets in artificial happiness and baby-moulding techniques will loom up. In the same way as unenforceable prohibition past a certain point probably eventually increased alcoholism and potsmoking, while robbing governments of respect, so America must be careful not to create Al Capones who bootleg genetic engineering. Worryingly, the 1975 world recession has caused a rush to train more pre-medic students and even doctors of chemistry than can possibly be employed; they might be the bootleg geneticists. At the other extreme, if legal controls over these approaching horrors are too mushy, changes in the nature of human beings may come about unchecked.

There can have been no period in history when it has been more crucial that the world's leading country should have lots of competing local governments, with a cool federal government sitting on top to decide from gradual experience which systems of adequate control look like working and which systems of overcontrol or no-control don't. The same is true for the reform that is now needed of life patterns. It is obvious that a lot of new experiments are needed to find how best to change society's present mishandling of children, adolescents (especially) and an increasing number of old people.

ENVOI

There are those who say that small-town America cannot possibly lead the world through these next few tumultuous years. They argue that the good-neighbourliness of American small towns, with everybody knowing everybody else, which the visiting foreigner still finds as the most civilised living pattern in the world, is the last harvest from the winning of the west by the madonna of the plains a hundred years ago. They agree that those who fled the villages and small towns in the nineteenth century, hating what Karl Marx called "the idiocy of rural life," may thankfully use the telecommuter revolution to flee back again from the idiocy of American city life. But they deny that Americans of this post-urban age will be well-placed to recreate the conditions whereby, to quote William Irwin Thompson, "mediaeval man dwelled in a village but lived in Christendom." (47)

They have two unflattering reasons. First, sophisticated Americans are running scared. Secondly, both simple and psychotic Americans have too often been dominated by religious liars. These points are worrying.

At this year's World Future Society assembly in Washington there were some people wandering around in a sort of robe from which dangled a convoluted cross. About half the audience found nothing shocking when one of them said from the platform:

Ecology is the first really moral science, because it says "Either you believe this, or you die."

After 2,000 years in which the great ethical advances brought to many societies by Christianity have been intermittently reversed into ethical retreats when zealots have threatened simple people with thunderbolts and eternal rotting in hell unless they believe even those parts of the Bible which every educated man knows to be fairy stories (most of them pinched from earlier religions anyway), half an audience of 2,000 very clever people in the capital of the world now laps up warnings from a fanatical fop that a similar sad fate will befall those who do not believe various schedules of certain commodities' elasticity of supply which any educated economist knows to be innumerate balderdash. At that moment I could see the arguments of those who say that America in its third century is as liable to lead the world back to the ignorance of the dark ages as into the knowledge-intensive age before us.

And yet, in the end, the truth is that in each of their half-a-dozen major crises since their first, when they seemed to have lost their revolution against the British in Valley Forge, the United States have done more wisely than any sane man at the time could reasonably forecast they would do.

There are three main questions. First, will America continue to believe in economic growth? Half the world will remain hungry if it does not, and that half-world may blow us up.

Second, should America believe in participatory producers' democracy in factory and politics, or in extended and informed consumers' freedom in both? Please God, it should believe in consumers' freedom.

Third, does the star-spangled banner still wave o'er the land of the free, and the home of the brave? The stars glitter, but no wise foreigner at this hour will rely wholly on George Washington's order of April, 1777: "Put none but Americans on guard tonight."

NOTES

1. A lot of the figures in this book are taken from contributions to *The Next 25 Years*, a book produced in conjunction with the World Future Society's second general assembly, June, 1975—obtainable from the World Future Society, 4916 St Elmo Avenue (Bethesda), Washington D.C. In *The Next 25 Years*, Herman Kahn's guess was "for world population stabilizing in the 21st century at about 15 billion, GWP/cap at about $20,000 and GWP at about $300 trillion, give or take factors of, say, two, three and four, respectively. In other words, population should be between 7 and 30 billion, GWP/cap between $5,000 and $60,000, GWP between $50 and $1,000 trillion." These figures were in 1974 dollars, whereas the figures I hazard all through this book are in second-half-of-1975 dollars. It is possible that my median guess is now a bit more optimistic than Herman Kahn's, but I do not think there is much difference between us. Herman Kahn is the pioneer in quantitative estimates of this kind (indeed, he was the first from whom I heard the term "gross world product"), and I am just an acolyte.

2. Anybody interested in this subject should read Gerald Leach's brilliant *The Biocrats* (Pelican Books), even though he will disagree with a lot of my later opinions in this book.

3. See J. K. Galbraith, *The New Industrial State* (Mentor Books).

4. The phrase "nearly 2 billion people on incomes under $200 a year with whom we share this rather small planet" or something like it, was used three times by zero-growth Americans in conversations with me. It was only after I had used the phrase in a rather snorting sense here that it was pointed out to me that it came from Lester Brown, and was indeed used in his contribution to *The Next 25 Years*, in another passage to which I refer in Note 25. Lester Brown, together with Gerald Leach and a few others, is one of the scholars on the other (the environmentalists') side of this argument whom I very much respect.

5. *The New York Times*, Feb. 1, 1931.

6. Figures plagiarized by me after a conversation with Herman Kahn. And it's in his contribution to *The Next 25 Years* too.

7. Reprinted in my brief booklet *The Next 40 Years, 1972–2012*, obtainable from *The Economist*, 25 St. James's Street, London SW1A 1HG.

8. "Why Growth Rates Differ," by Edward Denison.

9. From my *The Neurotic Trillionaire* (Harcourt Brace Jovanovich, Inc.).

10. Galbraith, *op cit.*

11. Yet another point I appropriated after conversation with Herman Kahn, plus a few embellishments of my own.

12. See John McHale *World Facts and Trends* (Collier-Macmillan). This is the first of many points (see below) to which my attention was drawn by this important work.

13. See my brief booklet *The Next 40 Years, 1972–2012, op cit.*

14. The phrase "confederations of entrepreneurs" first appeared in a position paper for the Diebold Institute of Public Policy Studies, which I do not think has ever been published. The basic ideas sprang from John Diebold, although I was one of those who worked with him in trying to fill them out. It is therefore probable that the ideas set down here accord more with my interpretation of what the concept ought to mean than with those of others in the discussions we held.

15. For the guesses in this and the next paragraph I am very much indebted to calculations set out in John McHale's *World Facts and Trends* (Collier-Macmillan).

16. I have used these figures several times (and have had checked that they are right), but I am still uncertain who first set them out. They were in my original notes for *The Next 40 Years*, but were not used then. Unfortunately the record I have now does not state the source.

17. I think that I first started this craze of comparing auto emissions to horse emissions in my booklet *The Next 40 Years*. But many others have taken it up more scientifically since. See Wilfred Beckerman *In Defence of Economic Growth* (Jonathan Cape), here quoting Professor Elliott Montrol.

18. See Herman Kahn in *The Next 25 Years*.

19. Beckerman, *op cit*.

20. This point is dealt with best in John McHale's *World Facts and Trends* (Collier-Macmillan), and also in John McHale's and Magda Cordell McHale's "Human Requirements, Supply Levels and Outer Bounds" (unpublished), which is a Policy Paper/Aspen Institute for Humanistic Studies Program obtainable from John McHale's Center for Integrated Studies at the State University of New York, at Binghamton.

21. See *Ocean Industry*, May 1969.

22. This is another passage in which I have drawn heavily on Herman Kahn's contribution to *The Next 40 Years*.

23. Beckerman, *op cit*.

24. Another point from John McHale's and Magda Cordell McHale's "Human Requirements, Supply Levels and Outer Bounds" (unpublished).

25. Any estimates for world population growth in 1974 still have to be very preliminary. But see Lester Brown's contribution to *The Next 25 Years* for confirmation of this guess.

26. Beckerman, *op cit*.

27. At the second general assembly of the World Future Society, Albert Adams presented a paper on "Aging in the USA," in which he proffered "an emerging 100-year self-actualisation and planned death model" for human lifetimes. I do not fully accord with this, but this sort of thinking should be taken seriously.

28. See John McHale's *World Facts and Trends* (Macmillan).

29. The terms "defense shift" and "welfare shift" were invented by Samuel Huntington (see "The Crisis of Democracy," a report to the Trilateral Commission).

30. See James Barber's brilliant paper on "Some Consequences of Pluralization in Government" in "The Future of the US Government," a report from the Commission on the Year 2000 of the American Academy of Arts and Sciences.

31. This crack is not original, but is quoted in the confidential report to which note 32 also refers.

32. See Note 31.

33. As with Note 14, these thoughts about performance contracts were formed while doing some work for the Diebold Institute of Public Policy Studies, with John Diebold himself as the principal originator. But he should not be blamed for all the side alleys up which my flights of fancy lead me on this subject.

34. See Alistair Cooke's *America* (BBC Publications).

35. See James Ramey's contribution to *The Next 25 Years*.

36. See Calvin Beale's very important paper on "Where are all the people going?" given to the 1975 Conference on Rural America.

37. See the paper presented by Laurence H. Day to the second general assembly of the World Future Society.

38. See Murray Turoff's "Potential Applications of Computer Conferencing in Developing Countries" presented at the 1974 Rome conference on futures research. Murray Turoff has done a lot of other work on computer conferencing. Peter Goldmark is a pioneer of ideas about telecommunications—supported rural communities (see "Communications Technology for Urban Improvement" in the 1971 report of the National Academy of Engineering's Committee on Telecommunications). And see also several of the publications of the Aspen Institute Program on Communicational Society, including a paper by Kas Kalba.

39. See Note 14 above. And see Simon Ramo's contribution to "A Look at Business in 1990," the White House 1972 conference on the "Industrial World Ahead."

40. See Calvin Beale, *op cit.*

41. See James Ramey's contribution to *The Next 25 Years*.

42. See Alvin Toffler's *Future Shock* (Random House).

43. See James Ramey's contribution to *The Next 25 Years* again.

44. This comparison was made in an editorial on a recent pop festival in the London *Daily Mail*.

45. See Laurence Day's paper, mentioned in Note 37.

46. This is another point made to me by Herman Kahn in private conversation.

47. See "Lindisfarne: A Planetary Community," in the February 1975 issue of *The Futurist*.

A 6
B 7
C 8
D 9
E 0
F 1
G 2
H 3
I 4
J 5